ONCE UPON A TIME IN HOLLYWOOD

Other Books by
Michael B. Druxman

Fiction
SHADOW WATCHER
(Novel)
NOBODY DROWNS IN MINERAL LAKE
(Novel)
CHEYENNE WARRIOR
(The Original Screenplay with Author Commentary)

Non-Fiction
FAMILY SECRET
(with Warren Hull)
THE ART STORYTELLING
THE MUSICAL: From Broadway to Hollywood
ONE GOOD FILM DESERVES ANOTHER
CHARLTON HESTON
MERV
MAKE IT AGAIN, SAM
BASIL RATHBONE: His Life and His Films
PAUL MUNI: His Life and His Films

Once Upon a Time in Hollywood

From the Secret Files of Harry Pennypacker

Michael B. Druxman

Once Upon a Time in Hollywood: From the Secret Files of Harry Pennypacker
© 2015 Michael B. Druxman. All Rights Reserved.

No part of this book may be reproduced in any form or by any means, electronic, mechanical, digital, photocopying or recording, except for the inclusion in a review, without permission in writing from the publisher.

Published in the USA by:
BearManor Media
PO Box 71426
Albany, Georgia 31708
www.bearmanormedia.com

ISBN 978-1-59393-790-4

Printed in the United States of America.

TABLE OF CONTENTS

Preamble vii
Introduction xi

I. John Wayne 1
II. Elvis Presley 17
III. James Dean 29
IV. Clark Gable 39
V. W. C. Fields & Mae West 55
VI. The Wizard of Oz 67
VII. The Marx Brothers 75
VIII. Marilyn Monroe 87

Postscript 95
Disclaimer 99
Acknowledgements 103
Dedication 107
About the Author 111

Preamble

★

Once upon a time in Hollywood
The major studios reigned supreme.
No actor, director nor lowly grip
Defied a Cohn or Mayer regime.

Once upon a time in Hollywood
Lies became the truth.
A hooker was made a lady fair
And truck drivers were given couth.

The stars were gods to be protected
Yet some were certainly dotty.
The fact is that Clark's pee-pee was small
And Marilyn definitely used the potty.

Tracy and Hepburn were just good friends
And Rock Hudson was a man among men.
When Bogart got into a barroom brawl,
Jack Warner screamed, "Not again!"

They tried to convince us that Rita could sing
And Flynn did all that derring-do
If you want to believe that, go right ahead
'Cause there's a bridge I'll be selling you.

Once upon a time in Hollywood
Dreams were turned to gold.
But those fortunes might have blown away
Had the real stories ever been told.

INTRODUCTION

★

What comes to you over the Internet never ceases to amaze me.

Almost daily, I receive e-mail offers to loan me thousands of dollars, give me a free plasma TV, meet beautiful single women from Russia, or enlarge my penis.

Occasionally, over the years, people who have a sensational story to relate have even contacted me and, since I am a storyteller by profession, I usually listen.

Most of these stories that come to me are worthless, but sometimes I do get a goodie.

Many years ago, a former Indiana police officer claimed to have met John Dillinger in the mid-1950s, approximately twenty years after the infamous outlaw was, ostensibly, shot down by FBI agents in front of Chicago's Biograph Theater.

I did some research and the result was my fictional movie *Dillinger and Capone* (1994), produced by Roger Corman and starring Martin Sheen and F. Murray Abraham.

More recently, I met a gent online named Warren Hull. He claimed to know who really murdered mobster Benjamin "Bugsy" Siegel in Beverly Hills in 1947. This led to our 2004 book, *Family Secret*.

About a year ago, a fellow named Stuart Blumberg approached me online. He was twenty-six years old, an aspiring filmmaker who was currently supporting himself working in the library of a major Los Angeles newspaper.

While sifting through some boxes in a storage room one day, Blumberg discovered the files of a deceased newspaper columnist named Harry Pennypacker.

According to Blumberg, for nearly fifty years Pennypacker was one of the top newspaper columnists in this country. He was a colleague of Walter Winchell and Louella Parsons, and he had national syndication in every major city.

I found that fact to be interesting, because I'd never heard of Pennypacker. I asked a couple of friends who worked at *The Hollywood Reporter* and *Daily Variety*, and they'd never heard of Pennypacker either.

Blumberg insisted the stuff that Pennypacker wrote about was sensational. Had it ever become public, Hollywood's history would have been totally revised.

Now, my interest was really piqued.

"So, why haven't I ever heard of this guy?" I asked Blumberg when we met for coffee at the Coffee Bean on La Cienega Boulevard.

"Because nobody ever ran his columns," Blumberg said. "He wrote 'em, but the editors killed them."

I studied this slightly overweight wannabe who was trying, somewhat unsuccessfully, to grow a beard and mustache on his boyish face, and began to wonder if I was talking to a screwball.

"I want to make a movie about him," Blumberg said, "and I figured that if a book came out first, getting financing would be easier."

"Okay," I said. "But, so far the only thing that you've told me is that nobody printed this guy's stories. Makes me wonder if he was a nut case, or even real"

"Harry Pennypacker was real, all right," Blumberg said, going on the defensive. "He was born in upstate New York on February 23rd, 1911."

"That's great," I said, finishing my coffee and getting ready to depart.

"I've got a recorded interview with Robert T. Atwater, his former editor," Blumberg said, producing a cassette player. "Would that convince you?"

"Let me hear it."

Blumberg said that he'd tracked down Atwater, who was then in his eighties, at Chicago's Old Newspaper Reporters Retirement Home. I would later try to call the Home to verify that Atwater once resided there, but I was told that the place had closed down because there were no longer any old newspaper reporters in Chicago.

What follows are actual quotes from Blumberg's alleged interview with the late Robert T. Atwater.

"Harry Pennypacker was a fine reporter. He could find a sensational news story under a rock, which is where he probably found most of his stuff.

"Over the years, he brought me some fantastic stories, like the one about Charles Lindbergh.

"Pennypacker came to me one day with 'proof' that Lindbergh never flew the Atlantic.

"That was a double who took off from the Long Island airfield. Lindbergh was already in England and, the next day, he got into his plane and flew across the Channel to Paris and to fame and fortune.

"Pennypacker got that story directly from Pieter Olafson, Lindbergh's double. He got him drunk one night in a bar and Olafson told him he was paid fifty dollars to fly that plane from Long Island to Chattanooga, Tennessee, then disappear.

"I killed the story. Lindbergh was a national hero. The country needed heroes.

"Besides, Olafson wasn't even around to verify his statement. When he wasn't flying planes, he worked in a circus. He was the guy that they shot out of a cannon.

"Two days after Pennypacker interviewed him, Olafson overshot the net, ricocheted off the Ferris wheel and crashed head first through the roof of the lion's cage.

"They could never tell if it was the fall that actually killed him.

"Pennypacker brought me more stories. Great stories. But, his stuff was so hot that we couldn't print it.

"We couldn't fire Pennypacker. He had an ironclad contact. So, we *transferred him to where his nose for sniffing out a scandal might be welcome.*

"*We sent him to Hollywood.*"

After listening to Atwater's words, I was hooked. Even if the Lindbergh story was only partially true, I felt that it deserved a public airing.

I spent the next two weeks reading Pennypacker's stories about Hollywood. Some of them were absolutely uncanny, but mesmerizing.

I wasn't sure if I really believed the material, but they were certainly good stories and, as I've told you, I am a storyteller.

Thus, I decided to help Blumberg put together this book, a combination of Harry Pennypacker's unfinished autobiography and some of his more intriguing columns, a revisionist history of Hollywood, and the icons who once resided there.

I can't vouch for the veracity of any of Pennypacker's stories, but they do make interesting reading.

Enjoy!

—Michael B. Druxman

Harry Pennypacker: He enjoyed the company of pigeons.

I
John Wayne

★

John Wayne!

He was America's most beloved hero, an on-screen symbol of this nation's strength.

More than a quarter century after his death, his films, like *Stagecoach, Red River, Sands of Iwo Jima, The Searchers, Rio Bravo* and *True Grit,* are still watched and revered by millions of fans throughout the world.

He was, indeed, a star whose brightness will never fade.

And yet, he did not exist.

That's right!

John Wayne was not real.

My name is Harry Pennypacker.

For nearly fifty years, I was one of the top newspaper columnists in this country. I had national syndication in every major city.

I know you've never heard of me.

That's because nobody ever ran my columns.

I wrote them, but the damn editors killed them.

Sure, I got paid. I had an ironclad contract.

But, my stuff was *so hot* that the papers were too scared to print it. They figured the truth would get the wrong people mad at them. They might lose some advertising.

They might even get sued.

You know what they made me do to justify my paycheck?

I had to write the goddamn TV listings:

"Tonight, on The Beverly Hillbillies, *Jed Clampett gets arrested in a Beverly Hills brothel by Sergeant Joe Friday of* Dragnet, *who was working undercover as one of the girls."*

Believe it or not, some of those listings were just that bad.

I've got the files for every *real* story I ever wrote, and I'm going to share some of them with you in this book, which should be a best-seller.

[God only knows that I can use the money.]

But, be warned!

What you are about to read may upset some of you. History is going to be rewritten and sacred icons destroyed.

Let me start by telling you about John Wayne.

Truthfully, I was very unhappy when I was assigned to cover Hollywood. The editors were just giving me simple bread-and-butter stories to cover, like interviewing celebrities at the opening of the latest Roy Rogers movie, or reviewing *Plan 9 From Outer Space*, the new film from director Ed Wood, Jr.

But, all that changed one day when I was at Warner Brothers Studios to interview Ronald Reagan's stand-in.

Actually, when I got to the studio, I found out that Ronald Reagan didn't have a stand-in, so I spent the morning walking around the lot, visiting some of the sets.

I was in the men's room, standing at one of the urinals, when who should take the spot next to me but John Wayne.

I was speechless. Here I was, standing next to one of America's greatest movie heroes, one of *my* heroes, taking a leak.

I'm only human. Like any other person, I was curious. So, when Wayne wasn't looking, I took a quick glance down and to the right.

What I saw shocked me. It shocked me so much that I screamed, jumped back and accidentally urinated on Wayne's pant leg.

I made a quick apology and ran out of the men's room. In fact, I ran to my car and drove out of the studio.

It took me awhile, but I realized that I had stumbled onto a story that could revolutionize my career.

I had found out that John Wayne was not real. There was no such person.

And, after months of research, I discovered that he was the creation of a brilliant unknown character actor named Mendel Skulnick.

This was one of the best-kept secrets in Hollywood.

If anyone knew, or even suspected the truth, they didn't say a word. They wouldn't dare.

You don't believe me?

Just look at some of the stunts that Wayne did on the screen.

Remember that bit in *True Grit* where he's riding across the field, reins in his teeth, shooting at the bad guys with a six-gun in one hand and a rifle in the other?

He even hit one or two of them.

That scene was ridiculous! Nobody could do that!

So, admit it! How could John Wayne be real?

The answer, of course, is he *wasn't* real.

How, you may ask, is all that possible?

How could Mendel Skulnick and Hollywood fool the movie-going public for nearly half a century?

The answer is very simple.

Make-up!

Mendel Skulnick was the greatest make-up artist in the history of motion pictures.

He could fool anybody.

He could disguise himself as men of all ages, shapes and sizes. Women of all ages, shapes and sizes. Children of all ages, shapes and sizes.

He could even become animals; cows, horses. Once he even became an alligator and almost bit a guy's leg off.

I'm telling you. Mendel Skulnick was a genius.

Of course, some of his disguises did have their disadvantages.

I'm thinking of the time he made himself up as an elm tree and attracted every dog in the neighborhood.

So, where did Mendel Skulnick come from, and how did he learn his uncanny skill for make-up?

That's another of Hollywood's well-kept secrets, one that I uncovered years ago at great danger to myself.

Mendel Skulnick was the illegitimate son of Lon Chaney, Sr.

Chaney, of course, was the greatest actor of the silent cinema. A make-up artist himself, he was the Hunchback of Notre Dame, the Phantom of the Opera.

He was the Man of 1000 Faces.

Unfortunately, Chaney could not give his son his name, so he passed on to him his great gift for disguise.

His magic make-up case.

Little Mendel's fascination with nature provided the inspiration for his earliest disguises.

However, he soon realized that some of these experiments were fraught with danger.

I mean, if you're going to disguise yourself as a spider, people are going to step on you, right?

Halloween was Mendel's favorite time of the year. That was when he could really let his imagination run wild. He loved to go trick-or-treating.

But, he was forced to stop that when his costumes began frightening the neighbors.

One Halloween alone there were three heart attacks and one stroke on his block.

How would you like to open your door and find an eight-foot tall Tyrannosaurus-Rex staring at you and licking his chops?

Mendel's mother, Sophie Skulnick, was a self-sufficient, Jewish woman with no family who immigrated to the United States from Czarist Russia in the early 1900s.

Like all people who came to this country, she believed that America was the land of opportunity.

She didn't like the big city, so, she took the advice of Horace Greeley, bought a ticket on the first train, and headed West.

"Go West, Young Woman!"

[Actually, Greeley said, "Go West, Young Man!" but who cares?]

At one point, the train was attacked by a band of marauding Cheyenne, but after Sophie made them a big pot of matzo ball soup and kreplach, the Cheyenne named her "Big Yiddishe Mama", made her an honorary member of their tribe and sent everybody on their way.

When they arrived in the bustling city of San Francisco, Sophie's fellow train passengers couldn't stop talking about how she had saved all of their scalps.

She was declared a heroine, but as she was being carried in triumph on the shoulders of several police and firemen, the ground beneath them began to shake.

At first, Sophie thought that the men who were carrying her were shikker, that they had been drinking. But, she was wrong.

Sophie had arrived in San Francisco just in time to experience the 1906 earthquake.

After the shaking had stopped and the fires were brought under control, Sophie emerged from the rubble and, once again, came to the aid of her fellow human beings.

Amid all the chaos of those first few days, Sophie Skulnick opened San Francisco's first kosher soup kitchen, serving people of all religions.

At night, she even knitted yarmulkes for Jews and gentiles alike. Anyone who had lost their own in the quake.

One of the people that Sophie helped back then was Abraham

Kaminsky. Before he passed away in 1963, I spoke with him and he recalled:

"Sophie Skulnick was a very good person. She served matzo ball soup and kuggle to many people after the San Francisco earthquake.

"Nobody knew where she got the stuff to make matzo ball soup and kuggle....We were afraid to ask.

"Actually, it didn't really taste like matzo ball soup and kuggle. It just looked like it.

"Actually, it didn't look like it either. But, Sophie Skulnick said it was matzo ball soup and kuggle.

"There wasn't anything else to eat, so we ate it....We didn't die.

"Sophie Skulnick was a very good person."

When San Francisco was rebuilt, Sophie Skulnick was there. She opened her own kosher delicatessen in the heart of that new city.

Sophie's was an instant success, not only as a fine eating establishment, but it soon became the city's premier caterer for weddings, bar mitzvahs, funerals and first communions.

Their knishes were to die for.

Sophie's had been open for a few years when, one day, actor Lon Chaney, who was visiting friends in San Francisco, wandered in to have lunch.

He ordered a bowl of matzo ball soup and the number seven on the menu, a double-decker corned beef/chopped liver sandwich on rye, topped off with a large kosher pickle.

As he bit into that huge sandwich, he spotted Sophie, standing by the cash register.

He couldn't take his eyes off of her, receiving the money from the customers, counting out their change. Chewing on his sandwich, he kept watching her, and he knew that he was in love.

This was the best goddamn corned beef/chopped liver sandwich he'd ever tasted.

Lon was desperate to meet this amazing woman. Anybody who could create such a sandwich had to be his.

When Lon Chaney paid his check that day, he looked into Sophie's eyes, and asked her for the secret of her corned beef and chopped liver.

She told him to go *shtup* himself.

But, Chaney wasn't a man who took "No" for an answer. He returned to Sophie's for dinner that night, then again for breakfast the next morning, then lunch and dinner again. And, he would always order the same thing: a bowl of matzo ball soup and the number seven.

In spite of herself, Sophie found Lon Chaney charming. She agreed to go out with him, providing that they didn't eat at a deli.

She was in the mood for Chinese.

To cut a long story short, Lon and Sophie hit it off. They kept seeing each other, day-after-day. Their affair was one of the world's great love stories, rivaling that of....

Samson and Delilah.

Romeo and Juliet.

Harold and Maude.

Even though Lon was married with a wife back in Los Angeles, the couple was inseparable. And then, one evening, Sophie told him: she was going to have a baby.

Lon offered to get a divorce and marry her, but there was a problem.

Actually, there were two problems. First, Lon wasn't Jewish.

"I'll convert," he said. "Anything not to lose you."

They discussed that possibility for a while, but after Lon learned that, in order to really become a Jew, he would have to undergo a certain operation on the lower part of his anatomy, he changed his mind.

But, there was another reason why Sophie didn't want to marry Lon.

Lon liked to work on his various make-ups late into the night. He often went to bed with them still on.

Can you imagine poor Sophie waking up in the middle of the night and finding the Phantom of the Opera lying next to her?

After the baby was born, Lon and Sophie parted and, even though he sent her money every month to help care for little Mendel, she still refused to give him the secret to her corned beef and chopped liver.

Sophie never forgot Lon. In fact, after he died in 1930, she changed the name of her restaurant to The Deli of 1000 Dishes.

Actually, there were only sixty-nine items on the menu, but who's counting?

Little Mendel was a quiet, lonely child, who loved cowboy movies. He saw just about every one that came out, because there was a silent movie theater down the block from Sophie's restaurant and, if he gave one of his mother's bagels to the doorman, he could get in free.

His hero was Dustin Farnum, star of Cecil B. DeMille's *The Squaw Man*. Mendel must've seen that movie twenty times.

For his fourth birthday, Sophie gave her son a cowboy outfit. That turned out to be a big mistake. Not only did little Mendel try to lasso every cat and dog in the neighborhood but, one day, he went into the restaurant and started lassoing the customers. He even had one old lady hog-tied before they were able to pull him off of her.

But, that didn't dissuade Little Mendel. He was going to be a cowboy hero like Dustin Farnum, Bronco Billy Anderson, William S. Hart, Tom Mix and Buck Jones.

With his trusty wooden hobbyhorse, Macher, he learned to ride.

With his slingshot, he also learned to shoot, and shoot well.

He became the terror of the neighborhood.

No window was safe.

But there was a problem. Mendel didn't have the physique or the looks to be a cowboy hero.

If he was going to be in western movies, he would have to be the comedy sidekick.

But, that was not for Mendel.

He wanted to do the daring deeds, catch the bad guys, and rescue the girl.

Sophie, of course, wanted him to take over the family business, but that was not to be.

Mendel was determined to be the next Tom Mix.

What happened to Dustin Farnum?

Why dress down in dusty old clothes like Dustin Farnum when you can dress up in clean, fancy duds like Tom Mix?

In the early 1930s, would-be actors were flocking to Hollywood from all over the country, and Mendel found door after door being slammed in his face.

Months went by. Living on the "care packages" of corned beef, pastrami, chopped liver and, of course, chicken soup that Sophie sent him every week, Mendel began to get discouraged. He even considered returning to San Francisco to join his mother in the restaurant business.

And, then it happened.

One afternoon, Mendel went to the movies, and the film he saw changed his life forever.

The movie was *Frankenstein* with Boris Karloff, the story of the mad scientist who created a living monster out of the body parts of human corpses.

The film fascinated Mendel. He stayed in the theater all day, watching showing after showing. In fact, when it came time for the theater to close for the night, Mendel hid in the men's room then slept in the auditorium so that he'd be there to catch the early show the next morning.

He did that for three straight days, surviving on popcorn, candy bars and soda pop.

Is it any wonder that his dentist made a small fortune off him that year?

But, it was worth it.

Mendel now knew how he would achieve his dream to become a cowboy hero in the movies.

Using what he'd gleaned from Dr. Frankenstein and also his father's magic make-up case, he would re-create himself as one.

No, he didn't go out and steal body parts from corpses. That would've been disgusting.

Besides, if he was going to create a new person, that person would have to be "durable", and everybody knows that, over time, a corpse....

Well, we don't need to go into that, do we?

Mendel's plan was brilliant! He was going to create the movies' first full-body suit.

To do this, he needed one key ingredient.

Rubber!

Mendel went out and bought every rubber ball he could lay his hands on.

He melted them down, molded them into prosthetic parts that would cover his entire body and then, using cloth joints, sewed the various parts together.

Mendel stepped into his prototype suit, had a friend zip up the back and, almost immediately, felt an urge to go to the bathroom.

It was then that he realized that he'd forgotten something.

His friend tried to unzip him, but the zipper wouldn't budge. It was stuck.

"Get a knife!" Mendel shouted. "Cut me out of it!"

The friend looked around, but there was no knife or scissors handy. They were all downstairs in Mendel's workroom, and the key was in his pocket inside the suit.

Two hours later, after the friend was able to cut him out of the prototype, Mendel took an immediate shower, and then he buried the suit.

The next prototype Mendel built had a trap door and a fly...but there were other problems.

As his neighbor, Emile Greenbaum, recalled when I interviewed him:

"Mendel was standing at the top of these stairs wearing this funny-looking suit, and he slipped.

"He came bouncing...bouncing...bouncing down the stairs, just like a bouncing ball.

"Damndest thing you ever saw.

"He was a little meshugge, but Mendel was a nice boy."

So, it was back to the drawing board. This time, Mendel sewed lead weights into the body suit, the feet, the legs, the butt.

That kind of explains why John Wayne always walked the way he did.

Once he had perfected his body suit, Mendel began working on a face for his cowboy hero.

Using prosthetics he'd created from his father's magic make-up kit, Mendel experimented for weeks until he came up with the look he wanted.

He practiced in front of a mirror to develop what would become his characteristic squint, his drawl, his on-screen persona. He even came up with the perfect catch-phrase:

"Now you listen, pilgrim, and listen good...."

And there he had it! A ruggedly handsome, no nonsense cowboy hero that women would swoon over and men would follow into any battle.

Now that his cowboy hero had a body and a face, all he needed was a name.

And, the name he chose was...Marion Morrison.

Don't ask.

A big strapping youth like Marion Morrison had no problem getting a job as a prop man at a Hollywood studio. It wasn't long before he caught the eye of director John Ford.

Ford saw a potential star in Mendel.

I mean, Marion.

But, the first thing he told him was that the name would have to go.

"No problem," said Mendel. "How about *Francis* Morrison?"

As the world knows, Marion Morrison became John Wayne..."the Duke"...and Mendel Skulnick virtually disappeared, though Sophie did get a card from him every Rosh Hashanah and, a couple of years later, she started doing the on-location catering for all of John Wayne's movies.

Just think of it. All those rough-and-tumble cowboy actors, horse wranglers and other goyim, out on the prairie, eating kuggle, kreplach and matzoh ball soup for lunch.

"The Duke" served his apprenticeship doing "B" westerns and serials....

But, it wasn't until his mentor, John Ford, cast him as The Ringo Kid in *Stagecoach* that his career really took off.

After that, he was America's hero; the screen's top action star, appearing not only in westerns, but also adventure films and war movies.

Actually, it was his war movies that proved somewhat embarrassing to the star.

People wanted to know why John Wayne wasn't in the military.

Following Pearl Harbor, Mendel did try to enlist. But, when it came time for the physical, he had to remove the body suit and that was that.

After the war, John Wayne continued to make movies, achieving virtual icon status and, in 1969, he won an Academy Award for his performance in *True Grit*.

I know what you're thinking. You're wondering how all this was possible. How, for over forty years, was Mendel able to disappear into John Wayne without the world finding out?

It's simple. Most people thought that Mendel was John Wayne's personal dresser. Although the fact that nobody ever saw both of them together did raise a few eyebrows.

I spoke to Rowdy Carpenter, a stunt man on several John Wayne movies, and he recalled:

"Every morning, you'd see this little guy go into Wayne's trailer, then a half-hour later, out would come the Duke...ready to work."

Then, there was Sadie Artoffski, the costume mistress on two Wayne pictures:

"He didn't fool me at all. One time, I had this shirt of his that needed mending. He was always fighting in his movies, so I always had to sew his shirts, his pants.

"I knocked on the door of his trailer. John Wayne told me to come in. I came in. John Wayne wasn't there. But, in the mirror, I could see into the bathroom. There was this little man in there, naked. And, he had the biggest shlong I've ever seen in my life.

"Who else could have a shlong that big but John Wayne?"

Obviously, she'd never seen Forrest Tucker, Milton Berle, Rock Hudson and, I don't like to brag, but...

Never mind.

The point is that, even if they knew, the actors and crew who worked on John Wayne's movies were wise enough to keep their mouths shut...*if* they wanted to keep working on John Wayne's movies.

As everybody knows, John Wayne had a family, several wives and children. So, I'll bet you're wondering, if John Wayne wasn't real, where did this family come from?

They came from Central Casting, the service that supplies extras to the movie studios. These were extras who were willing to make a life-long commitment to their new roles.

John Wayne was a valuable commodity. The studios had to protect their star. The publicity department created an entirely new background for him.

They even made him a star football player at USC.
Mendel was 5'6" and 150 pounds.
Can you imagine him playing football at USC?
Can you imagine him playing football anywhere?

So, there you have it...the real story of John Wayne.
What happened to Mendel?
He died in 1979...the same year that we lost John Wayne.
Mendel's body was placed inside his famous body suit...then bronzed.

You can visit him any time in Los Angeles outside the Larry Flynt Building on Wilshire Boulevard at La Cienega.*

---

* As this book goes to press, there are rumors circulating that the John Wayne bronze may be moved from its present location to somewhere in politically conservative Orange County.

I think Mendel and "the Duke" would like that.

II
Elvis Presley

★

I was disappointed when the newspaper refused to print my John Wayne story.

But, my editor told me that even more than Charles Lindbergh, John Wayne was an icon, a national hero.

How could he print my story and destroy that image?

I was furious, so I did what any good reporter would do in the same situation.

I went on a drunken bender.

When I woke up, I found myself in Mexico, singing and playing guitar in a local bar.

I had no idea how I got there and I had even less idea of why I was playing guitar and singing...since I'd never sung a note before in my life.

That might explain why the customers were throwing empty beer bottles at me.

But, it was in that bar that I met Oscar Agnew, the man who gave me the tip for one of the biggest stories of my career.

Interesting, isn't it, that I met so many of my sources in bars?

Before Oscar Agnew had moved to Mexico and taken up residence in the local bar, he'd lived in Los Angeles where he'd worked as a recording engineer at a small, out-of-the-way sound studio. He was also a member of his church choir.

One day, at work, Oscar was assigned a midnight recording session. Oscar didn't like to work that late, but the regular man was sick.

"Who are we recording?" he wanted to know, but his boss wouldn't tell him.

When the recording artist walked into the studio that night, Oscar nearly fell off of his chair.

Actually, he did fall off of his chair, but that's beside the point.

He recognized the man as a member of his church choir and, naturally, the man recognized him, also.

There were two minutes of screaming, shouting and, five minutes later, Oscar was fired from his job.

He was given five thousand dollars in cash and told, if he knew what was good for him, he'd get out of town and never tell anybody what he'd just seen.

Five years later, I met Oscar in that Mexican bar. The five thousand dollars was gone, so figuring that he had nothing to lose and, since I was buying the drinks, he told me his story.

What was it that got him fired and run out of Los Angeles?

This is his story, pretty much the way that I originally wrote it:

If John Wayne was "the Duke", then he was "the King". The King of Rock-and-Roll.

For more than a quarter century, he thrilled his audiences gyrating to hit tunes like "Hound Dog", "Blue Suede Shoes", "Love Me Tender", "Jailhouse Rock", and "Viva Las Vegas". His movies had teens and young adults from all over the world dancing in the aisles. And, his live concerts caused near riots wherever he appeared.

His name was Elvis Presley...and, the truth is that he couldn't sing a note.

How could that be possible?

Meet Otis Washington. He was the *real* Elvis Presley.

That's right, Otis Washington was the man who walked into Oscar Agnew's recording studio that night.

After an exhaustive search, I traced Mr. Washington to his home in South Central Los Angeles.

But, this story doesn't start with Otis Washington. It begins with Colonel Tom Parker.

Colonel Tom Parker was as much a colonel as I am a brain surgeon.

For all I know he was really a private.

"Colonel" was an honorary title, bestowed on him by several governors of Southern states.

Don't ask me why.

Back in the 1930s and 40s, Parker worked in carnivals, probably as a snake oil salesman.

Eventually, he started booking country-western acts, like Gene Austin, Hank Snow and Eddy Arnold.

It was around the early 1950s that he first met Otis Washington.

Otis was a tall, lanky African-American in his late twenties. He worked in a gas station outside of Nashville, Tennessee.

One day, Parker pulled into that station to fill up his tank and Otis waited on him. And, while Otis was checking under Parker's hood, the young man started singing to himself, "Swing Low, Sweet Chariot" to a boogie beat.

As Washington recalled when I interviewed him:

"The Colonel, he come up to me and say, 'Boy...'"

"He always called me 'Boy'. Fact is, the Colonel called most everyone 'Boy'.

"Anyway, he say to me, 'Is that you singin'?'

"I say, 'Yes, sir, that's me.'

"He say, 'Where'd an ugly son-of-a-bitch like you get a beautiful singin' voice like that?'

"I say, 'The good Lord give it to me, sir. I sing in church every Sunday.'

"He say, 'To a boogie beat!?!'"

Parker knew that he had something with Washington and his unique way of styling a song.

At least, he had *half* of something.

The problem was that Otis *was* an ugly son-of-a-bitch and, whereas he might have a stellar career as a radio and recording artist, the minute the public got a look at him, that career would be over.

Now, if the Colonel could only marry that voice to another body... .

Then, he remembered... .

A few weeks earlier, Parker had been in Memphis and been asked to judge a hula-hoop contest. At first, he said there was no way in holy hell that he'd sit and watch a bunch of stupid kids wiggle their asses, but when they offered him a case of Jim Beam and a box of Havana cigars, he relented.

There had been one wiggling ass that had caught the Colonel's eye.

No, it didn't belong to a girl and, no, the Colonel wasn't gay.

That wiggling tush belonged to a young man named....

That's right! Elvis Presley.

The way Elvis gyrated his hips in that hula-hoop was absolutely sensual; erotic.

The Colonel studied the crowd and noticed that the young girls couldn't keep their eyes off of Elvis and his gyrating tush.

As Ethel Mae Simpson, a grandmother now who went to high school with Elvis, recalled:

"All the girls at school were just crazy about Elvis. He had the cutest butt, and we loved it when he wore those tight jeans of his."

But, good looks and a cute butt do not a star make, as Parker soon found out.

After the hula-hoop contest, which, incidentally, Elvis won, the Colonel took the young man aside and asked, "Can you sing, boy?"

And, Elvis replied, in his high squeaky voice, "Yes, sir, I can."

That's the truth.

Elvis sounded like a cross between Mighty Mouse and a eunuch.

Kinda shocking, isn't it?

Recalls Ethel Mae:

"Elvis had a wonderful voice. He sang falsetto in all our school plays."

The Colonel sighed, slapped Elvis on the back and wished him luck, then left. He'd put him completely out of his mind until that day he'd stopped to get gas and met Otis Washington.

And, then a light bulb went off in the Colonel's head.

What if Otis Washington's voice could be married to Elvis Presley's good looks and gyrating tush?

Otis Washington: *"That was the stupidest thing I'd ever heard in my life."*

But Colonel Parker was not to be deterred. He knew that he had a potential gold mine with these two young men. He decided to bring them together.

That historic meeting took place over a sumptuous meal of fried chicken, mashed potatoes and gravy at the Kentucky Fried Chicken restaurant in Memphis, Tennessee.

[I wonder if I can get KFC to pay me for a commercial plug on that.]

Not much was said at the start of that meeting. The three men just ate their meal in silence. Then, Elvis spoke up. "Mind if I have another order of mashed potatoes, Colonel?" he asked.

Otis Washington: *"Elvis, he loved them mashed potatoes. How do ya' think he got so fat later on?"*

Finally, after a third helping of mashed potatoes, the three men got down to business.

What the Colonel proposed is that he could make Elvis a major star...*if* they used his body on stage and Otis Washington's voice off-stage.

Otis Washington: *"I asked the Colonel, how we could do that? People'd know Elvis was singin' to a record. An' the Colonel say, 'We ain't gonna use no record. You're gonna be backstage, singin' live.'*

"I looked at the Colonel and thought, 'You're a goddamn motherfuckin' fool.' But, I didn't say that. If I did, he might not've bought us desert."

Back in his carnival days, Colonel Parker had learned a valuable skill...hypnotism.

It was his idea to hypnotize both Otis and Elvis to be "in-sync", so that when they spoke or sang, they would speak or sing as one.

Otis Washington: *"When he told me that, I knew he was crazy."*

Then, Parker offered Otis $75.00 per week.

Otis Washington: *"What's wrong with being crazy?*

"Seventy-five dollars a week was a hell of a lot more than I was makin' at the gas station. It was a hell of a lot more than my boss was makin'."

The hypnotism sessions began, first with Elvis, then with Otis and finally both together.

The three men worked long, hard grueling hours that became days and more days. Sometimes tempers were short.

Then, after three months of rehearsal, they were ready for their first public performance.

Unfortunately, that first performance was an absolute disaster.

Otis Washington: *"I was singin' two bars faster than him, then I'd slow down and, instead of speedin' up, he'd slow down, too.*

"The people out front started booing, throwin' pop bottles at the stage. I was sure glad that I wasn't out front. Otherwise, I might've wound up with a bump on my head, too."

More rehearsals.

Days...weeks...months together.

Remember, the goal was for Elvis and Otis to speak and sing as one.

It's also rumored that, during this period, when Elvis was under deep hypnosis, he signed that infamous management agreement that gave the Colonel half of his future earnings.

Otis Washington: *"I liked Elvis. He was a nice fella. But, you gotta admit that he was a bit of a smuck.*

"Is that right? Is it smuck, or shmuck?"

The next time that Elvis appeared on stage, he was a sensation. The women went wild with his gyrating hips and deep sexy voice.

Otis Washington: *"My voice."*

Virtually overnight, Elvis became the hottest star in show business, earning millions in personal appearances, record sales, movies and merchandising.

Otis Washington: *"And, I'm earning $75.00 a week."*

Once Elvis became a star, Otis Washington went to Colonel Parker and demanded a raise. The Colonel was a fair-minded, generous man. He doubled Otis' salary.

Otis Washington: *"That sumbitch gave me $150.00 dollars a week.*

"Bullshit!

"You know what I did?

"I got laryngitis

"Couldn't sing for days...weeks

"Colonel finally asked me how much it would cost to cure me...permanently.

"I said, '$5000 a week should do it.'

"He give me a nasty look, an' say 'Done.'

"I ain't no smuck.

"Shmuck?

"Actually, you say it your way and, for $5000 a week, I'll say it mine."

Keeping Otis Washington happy was one thing. Keeping his existence a secret was a little more difficult.

That's why Oscar Agnew wound up in Mexico.

Otis Washington: *"I knew Oscar from church. He was the biggest damn blabber-mouth you'd ever want to meet.*

"He'd see or hear somethin' one minute and an' it'd come out of his mouth the next, faster than shit through a goose.

"Hell, he had to go.

"Anyway, they'd sneak me into a recording studio every night with the script pages Elvis had to film the next day. I'd pre-record his dialogue and his songs.

"That was my voice you heard up on the screen, not his."

Angie O'Neill, an actress in one of Presley's movies, recalled: *"The Colonel wouldn't let the director change a line of dialogue, and Elvis said his lines exactly the same way, take after take."*

And Bill Baston, a grip on several of the movies, said: *"Elvis didn't talk much when he was off-camera, and when he did, his voice didn't sound the same.*

"Actually, The Colonel did most of his talking for him."

The truth is that, if you wanted to work on an Elvis Presley movie or recording session, you had to sign an iron-clad confidentiality agreement...in blood.

Elvis died in 1977 and the Colonel met his maker...not sure if that was upstairs or downstairs...twenty years later.

Washington was in his seventies when I talked to him. His health was failing and he used a walker. He was living in a small house with a part-time caregiver. He spoke to me because, before he died, he wanted the truth to be known.

Otis Washington: *"After the Colonel died, those $5000 a week checks stopped....I'm not gonna be 'round much longer, so I figured I'd set the record straight. That's why I'm talkin' to you."*

One thing I was curious about.

Washington had made over a quarter million a year working for Presley and the Colonel, but now he was living very modestly. I wanted to know what had happened to all his money.

Otis Washinton: *"My four ex-wives got a lot of it.*

"Then, I made some bad investments.

"When the home video thing started back in the 1970s, I figured I'd get in on the ground floor. Opened up a chain of video rental stores across the country.

"Unfortunately, I stocked them all with Beta."

And, that's the true story of Elvis Presley. First-rate journalism, if I do say so myself.

But, the story was never printed. Once again, my editor killed it.

He said that Elvis might've been dead, but he was still earning millions for the studios and the Colonel.

How could we kill such a cash cow?

III

JAMES DEAN

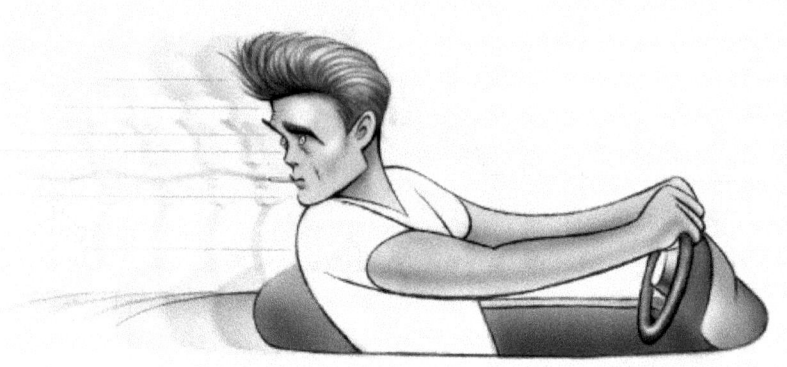

★

After they killed my Presley story, I fell into a deep depression.

I was almost suicidal.

But, rather than blowing my brains out, I did the next best thing.

I went to Las Vegas.

I drank.

I gambled.

I visited the Mustang Ranch.

I brooded.

I visited the Mustang Ranch.

And, while I was playing blackjack one night at the Flamingo, I met another gent who was in Vegas trying to forget: Dr. Sam Hoffman, a plastic surgeon from Walla Walla, Washington.

Dr. Sam had recently lost his license to practice medicine, the result of one too many of his experimental operations going wrong.

He'd discovered, much to the dismay of his patient, that he could *not* enlarge a human penis by transplanting the member of a recently excited horse.

After Dr. Sam related his sad story, I made the disgraced doctor aware of my troubles.

I took a drink and told him about Lindbergh.

I took another drink and told him about John Wayne.

I finished the bottle, and then told him about Elvis.

"I think I have a solution to your problem," Dr. Sam said.

"Oh," I replied.

Dr. Sam nodded. "Have I got a story for you."

"What is it?" I asked, my mouth drooling.

[Okay, It wasn't really drooling.]

"I can't tell you the actual story," Dr. Sam said. "If I did, I'd get my ass sued and maybe even get put in jail...if they didn't kill me first.

"But, I'll give you a date. It's a very famous date. You investigate what happened on that date and you'll uncover the best kept secret in Hollywood."

I shrugged, and then figuring I had nothing to lose, asked, "What's the date?"

Dr. Sam lowered his voice, "September 30th, 1955," he said.

I thought for a minute, then asked, "Why would the date my divorce became final be the best kept secret in Hollywood?"

Once I realized that other events also took place on that date, I began to do some checking, and when I came up with the particular event that Dr. Sam was talking about, I....

Well, once again, here's the way I pretty much wrote it.

Hollywood, as we've learned, is a town of deep, closely held secrets. And, when those secrets involve movie stars who are multi-billion dollar cash cows, then agents, personal managers and the studios will stop at virtually nothing to protect their interests.

Perhaps the strangest story of this sort to come out of Hollywood involved actor James Dean.

He starred in only three motion pictures...*East of Eden, Rebel Without a Cause* and *Giant*, yet he became the icon for an entire generation of rebellious youth, angered and frustrated by the confusing world in which they lived.

And, all this happened after he was dead.

James Dean died in a car crash on September 30th, 1955, shortly after filming his final scenes on *Giant*...and just a few weeks before the release of his second movie, *Rebel Without a Cause*.

But, did James Dean *really* die in that crash?

Or, was the accident the start of still another conspiracy to create a Hollywood money machine?

The truth is that James Dean did *not* die in that crash. In fact, he kept making movies for years afterwards.

I tracked down Anthony Ricardo, former publicist at Warner Brothers. He currently lives in Tuscon, Arizona, with his wife, Paul Grayson.

What Tony told me made my hair stand on end.

"The first reports said that Jimmy had been killed in the crash, but that was a mistake.

"He'd been banged-up quite a bit. Some bad cuts, bruises, a couple of broken bones.

"Oh, that poor beautiful face.

"He was in a coma, but the doctors expected him to come out of it.

"I was about to put out an announcement that he was still alive when I got a call from Jack Warner."

As the head of Warner Brothers Pictures, Jack Warner was worried.

The studio had a lot of money tied up in James Dean. *East of Eden* had done well at the box-office, but Warner secretly considered *Rebel Without a Cause* to be "just another stupid juvenile delinquent movie that would be lucky to break even."

What he was *really* concerned about was *Giant*.

The studio had a small fortune invested in that film and the early rushes that Warner had seen were not what he'd expected.

Former Warner Brothers executive, Alan Picard: *"When George Stevens pitched* Giant *to Jack, all Jack heard was the word 'Texas', and he figured he'd be making a western...not a romantic drama that stretched over several generations.*

"I remember, he came out of the screening room and he was in shock.

"He said, 'What is this movie? Liz Taylor and Rock Hudson are hugging, kissing and talking....

"'Dean is covered in oil, mooning over Liz. You can't even see his goddamn face.

"'I thought we were making a western.

"'Where're the Indians? The gunfights?

"'Where are John Ford and John Wayne when you need them?'"

Anthony Ricardo: "Mr. Warner said to me: 'Don't put out the release.'

"I said, 'Sir, James Dean is alive. We have to let people know.'

"'Why?' he said. 'He's more valuable to us dead. Remember Valentino?'"

Warner was, of course, referring to Rudolph Valentino, the famous silent screen idol whose sudden untimely death resulted in a near riot at his funeral and annual graveside tributes that are held to this very day.

Anthony Ricardo: "'Mr. Warner,' I said, *'you're not suggesting that we kill him, are you?'*

"'Noooo,' he said after a pause. A rather long pause. 'That would be murder and that would be wrong.

"'Let's just say he's dead and make him disappear.'

"'What if he objects?' I said.

"'Fuck 'im,' Warner said. 'I got an iron-clad contract with that little son-of-a-bitch and he'll do what I say.'"

And so, the plot was hatched. While the world mourned the passing of James Dean, the young actor was moved to a small private sanitarium outside of Walla Walla, Washington, where he took the next several months to recover.

Extensive plastic surgery was even performed on his face to insure he wouldn't be recognized.

Guess who they got to perform the operation.

That's right! Doctor Sam.

When Dean objected to the operation, a studio lawyer showed him a copy of the contract he'd signed that gave Warner Brothers complete control over his life for the next seven years.

Anthony Ricardo: *"The irony is that* Rebel Without a Cause *and* Giant *became two of the biggest hits that the studio ever had...and James Dean became the biggest star in the business.*

"But he was 'dead', even though he was really alive in a sanitarium up in Washington State.

"Warner was kicking himself. He had a half-dozen scripts that were perfect for Dean, but he couldn't use him.

"One day he called me into his office. Said: 'I know what we'll do with James Dean. We'll remake him.'

"'Remake him?' I asked.

"'Yeah, we remake movies. Why not actors?

"'He's got a new face, doesn't he? I even got the perfect name for him... Troy Donohue.'

"'Excuse me, Mr. Warner,' I said. 'We just gave that name to one of our new contract players.'

"He grunted, thought for a minute, then said: 'What about Tab Hunter? He's not signed with us any more. Does he own his name or do we?'"

Unfortunately, there was another factor that threatened the re-making of James Dean.

Alan Picard: *"I don't know who they got to do Jimmy's plastic surgery up in Washington, but the guy really botched it.*

"To be fair, you have to put some of the blame on Jack Warner. Before they did the operation, the doctor asked Jack what kind of new face he wanted Jimmy to have.

"Jack was kinda busy that day, so he blew him off. Said: 'Use your own judgment. Just make him look interesting.'

"Turns out this doctor liked to experiment. He was also a science-fiction buff.

"His favorite movies were Them! and The Beast From 20,000 Fathoms.

"Both Warner Brothers pictures, I might add.

"I'm sure that his surgery was inspired by his love for those movies.

"What he did to Jimmy's face... I don't even want to talk about it."

So, now, instead of a young talented leading man on their payroll, Warner Brothers had a young Boris Karloff... except that audiences weren't buying horror movies in the 1950s. They wanted science-fiction. Frankenstein was out and The Creature from the Black Lagoon was in.

Alan Picard: "'So, we'll cast him in sci-fi movies,' Warner said. 'The truth is, I never cared much for the kid's style of acting anyway. He's a mumbler. Half the time, you can't even understand 'im.

"'One Marlon Brando in this town is enough.'"

James Dean's first assignment when he returned to the studio with his new face was *The Black Scorpion*, a science-fiction thriller that featured giant, man-eating insects.

He played the title role.

That should give you some idea of how bad his plastic surgery was.

After that, Warner started loaning Jimmy out to various independent producers who specialized in low budget sci-fi movies. He never received billing, but over the next few years, he played the title role in a dozen or so of those Poverty Row epics.

One of those low budget producers was Conrad Rogers, who specialized in movies about atomic age monsters and aliens from outer space.

Conrad Rogers: *"Jimmy brought a sensitivity to his monsters. They were multi-dimensional performances, like the ones he gave in* East of Eden *and* Rebel Without a Cause.

"*I know that's hard to believe, but judge for yourself. Take a look at my films,* The Creature From Planet Zero, Son of The Creature From Planet Zero, *or even better,* The Slasher Beast from Mars. *All three are available on home video.*

"*Jimmy played the title role in all three of those cult classics.*

"*Just compare his performances in my films to what he did in, say* Rebel Without a Cause, *and you'll have to agree that he exhibited the same style, the same depth of feeling that he had in that picture.*

"*The scenes in which he ripped his victims apart and devoured their intestines were absolutely brilliant.*

"*If they gave Oscars to actors in horror films, Jimmy would have had a shelf full of them.*"

Actually, around Hollywood there *was* talk about giving Jimmy a special Academy Award for his in-depth portrayals of giant bugs and grotesque space monsters.

And then, tragically, fate intervened once more.

Conrad Rogers: "*We were shooting this space movie. Jimmy was playing a giant 'blob' from Mars, Uranus or one of those other planets.... Wherever blobs come from.*

"*Anyway, the prop man screwed up.*

"*He was supposed to load the ray gun with blanks, but he'd been out boozing it up the night before and he put real rays into the gun.*

"*It was terrible.*

"*The hero.... I don't remember if it was Richard Carlson or John Agar. They were both saving the world from space monsters back then.*

"*Which ever one it was....*

"*Right on cue, he fired the ray gun at Jimmy and disintegrated him on the spot.*

"All that was left was the zipper from the back of his blob costume.

"Thank God we got the shot. It would've cost a goddamn fortune if we had to re-shoot."

Alan Picard: *"Jack Warner was furious about what had happened to Jimmy.*

"The studio had been making a small fortune in loan-out fees for Dean's services on those sci-fi films and, now that source of income was lost to the studio forever.

"Jack wanted to sue the producer, but then he realized that the truth of what really happened to Jimmy might come out in court, so he dropped it.

"One thing that he did do was to insist that the prop man be blacklisted. The poor guy never worked in this town again.

"I hear he got a job with the Defense Department...in Weapons Development."

There was no funeral or memorial service this time. After all, James Dean had died on September 30th, 1955.

However, a few weeks after the ray gun accident, rumor has it that one of the actor's close friends journeyed back to Dean's home state of Indiana where he's supposedly buried and laid that zipper on top of the stone grave marker.

It remained there for a few days until a seamstress, visiting her mother's grave, absconded with it to use in a new evening dress that she was making.

James Dean: Two careers. Two deaths. One legend.

I like that: *"Two careers. Two deaths. One legend."* Not bad.

Too bad my editor didn't agree.

You know why this story got killed?

It was Jack Warner.

He called the editor personally, begged him to kill it, and then wound up making a large contribution to the editor's favorite charity.

That would be his retirement fund.

IV

CLARK GABLE

★

Perhaps Hollywood's greatest love story is that of Clark Gable and Carole Lombard.

He was the "King of Hollywood", and she was the "Queen of Screwball Comedy".

Books and even movies have told of their legendary romance and marriage, which tragically ended shortly after America's entry into World War II when Carole was killed in a plane crash just outside of Las Vegas, Nevada.

They say that Clark never really recovered from Carole's death.

And yet, it was all a sham.

Because, Carole Lombard was Clark Gable's "beard".

No, Clark Gable wasn't gay. There were certainly enough ladies in and out of Hollywood who could attest to that fact.

True, he may have had a little pee-pee.

[I saw him once in the locker room.]

But, that's beside the point.

Getting back to the main issue:

Clark Gable and Carole Lombard were the best of friends, but he was in love with somebody else.

It was a forbidden love that nobody dared talk about.

Carole knew very well that Clark loved another, but she was a good sport about it.

In fact, she got a kick out of playing Clark's "beard".

When MGM's Louis B. Mayer got wind of the romance, he almost had a heart attack.

When he heard that I knew about the affair, he threatened to put out a contract on my life if the story ever saw print.

David O. Selznick, producer of *Gone With the Wind*, offered to take the contract.

So, who was this person that Hollywood's biggest star had fallen hard for, and why did the relationship have these movie moguls so frightened?

She was an actress who Clark had worked with previously on both *China Seas* and *Saratoga*.

No, it wasn't Jean Harlow, his co-star in those two films.

You'll recall that she died before *Saratoga* had finished filming.

This actress was a supporting player who would achieve her greatest fame for her performance in *Gone With the Wind*.

No, it wasn't Vivien Leigh.

She was involved with Laurence Olivier. Remember?

And, it wasn't Olivia de Havilland.

Give up?

Okay, sit down and hold onto your hats.

Clark Gable and Hattie McDaniel were lovers.

That's right, Rhett Butler and Mammy got together long before they made *Gone With the Wind*.

Gable may have been married to Carole Lombard, but he really loved his Mammy, all two hundred pounds of her.

Maybe it was because his own real mother died when he was a baby. I don't know.

How did I learn all this?

I got the information from Miss Matilda Webster. She was an extra on *Gone With the Wind*. She played one of the plantation slaves, and she was also a close personal friend of Hattie McDaniel.

When Matty wasn't working as an extra, she made her living as a domestic. I had her in to clean my apartment once a week.

She was a skinny, sassy lady and very out-spoken. "Mr. Harry," she'd say to me, shaking her finger, "didn't your Mama ever teach you nuthin'? Didn't she teach you not to pile up your dishes in the sink or to pick your clothes up off the floor?"

Matty was great. I loved that lady.

Every now and then, she'd come in early, wake me up. "Get your no-account lazy tuchis out of bed," she'd say slapping me on the backside.

[Two days a week she worked for a Jewish family. That's were she learned words like "tuchis", "chutzpa", and, most importantly, "oy".]

Despite my usual hangover, I'd roll out of bed, shower, and then she'd make me breakfast. We'd sit across the table from each other, drinking coffee (sometimes with a shot of bourbon in it), schmoozing, and, one day, she told me about Clark and Hattie.

"Hattie had a boyfriend back in the 1920s and 30s," she said. "A white boy."

"No kiddin'," I said. "That must've raised some eyebrows."

"They kept it pretty secret," she said. "Never went no place together. Just sorta kept to themselves.

"I just saw him once, drivin' away in his Duesenberg."

"He was driving a Duesenberg?" I said, nearly choking on my coffee.

"I think it was a Duesenberg. Big one."

"What'd he look like?"

"I didn't really get a good look at him. It was night. But, he was a tall, good lookin' fella. A regular Rhett Butler."

Was Matty trying to tell me something?

I knew that Clark Gable once drove a Duesenberg.

And, what was that "Rhett Butler" remark if not a hint?

"You're saying that she was sleeping with Clark Gable?" I said.

"I didn't say that," she snapped.

"You *did* say he was 'a regular Rhett Butler'."

"I meant, he was a Rhett Butler *type*," she said. "Like Gary Cooper. He's a Rhett Butler type, too."

Now, I was really getting confused, because I knew that Gary Cooper also once drove a Duesenberg.

"You're saying that she was sleeping with Gable *and* Cooper?" I said.

"I ain't saying nuthin' more," she interrupted. "I don't know who it was, 'cept he did have a mustache."

That eliminated Cooper. So, now we *were* talking about Gable.

"Come on, Matty," I coaxed. Tell me. It's worth twenty bucks."

"I wouldn't tell you for fifty," she said, "'cause I don't really know."

"Matty," I said, staring her square in the eye for a good sixty seconds. "Tell me."

"All I know is that they may have had a child together," she finally said. "A little boy."

"Wow!" I said. "Gable had a child with her?"

"I never said it was Gable. And, I never said, for sure, that she had a baby."

"Well, what *are* you saying?"

"You know, you really give me a lot of *tsuris*, Mr. Harry."

["Tsuris". That's another word she picked up from her Jewish family.]

"What makes you think Hattie had a baby?" I persisted.

"She went away for a few months, somewhere down South," Matty said. "When she came back, she had this little boy child with her. Cutest thing you ever saw."

"How did she explain it?"

"She said it belonged to a friend of hers that died, but I always kinda wondered 'bout that."

"What happened to the boy?"

"Hattie put him up for adoption. What else could she do? If it *was* hers, that white man wasn't going to marry her."

"Of course not," I said. "That would have been unthinkable back then. Career suicide."

"You keep talkin' like the man was Clark Gable," Matty snapped, getting up from the table. "I told you, I don't know who it was. For all I know, the guy could have worked in a gas station."

"And he drove a Duesenberg?" I quipped.

"Maybe he borrowed it one night from a customer. I don't know."

She grabbed a mop and stomped out of the room. I followed her.

"Just one more question," I said, as she started to clean the bathroom.

"What?"

"Who adopted the child?"

"I don't know. Family named 'Davis', I think."

I started putting the pieces of the puzzle together.

I knew that Clark Gable had known Hattie McDaniel for years, and their scenes together in *Gone With the Wind* revealed a genuine affection between them.

I knew that Gable had a Duesenberg.

I knew that Gable had a mustache.

I knew that Gable was white.

He was also Rhett Butler.

Hattie McDaniel's boyfriend was white, had a mustache, drove a Duesenberg and was "a regular Rhett Butler".

He *had* to be Clark Gable.

I called Howard Strickling, head of MGM publicity. If anybody knew where the bodies were buried, it was Howard.

"Are you insane?" he said, after I told him what I'd discovered. "That's the most ridiculous thing I've ever heard in my life."

Then, he started laughing uncontrollably and hung up.

Howard's abruptness pissed me off, but then I realized that his denial was actually his way of telling me that I was on the right track.

After all, he certainly wasn't going to admit to me that Gable had a love child, and a black one at that.

Now, if I could only find the kid, I would have positive proof that my story was true.

The problem was that "Davis" is a very common name.

Where do I start?

Years went by. Hattie McDaniel was dead. Gable was dead. Mayer was dead. Selznick had been retired for years.

One night, shortly after my James Dean story went into the toilet, Jim Beam and I were sitting in my apartment watching television, and there was the kid on the tube right in front of me.

He was on some variety show, singing, dancing and doing impressions of famous people, Edward G. Robinson, Jimmy Cagney and Clark Gable.

His Gable impression was perfect. It was so good that, even though this kid was black, I thought that I was watching the real Clark Gable.

So, who was this kid?

His name was Sammy Davis, Jr.

Davis!

It all fit.

How else could he do such a great Clark Gable impersonation if it wasn't in his genes?

And, he had a mustache.

I tracked down Sammy Davis. Showed up unannounced at his home in Beverly Hills one night.

Sammy was hosting a dinner party. Frank Sinatra was there. So was Dean Martin.

When Sammy came to the door, I came right to the point. "Mr.

Davis," I said, "did you know that Clark Gable was your real father?"

He looked at me like I was crazy. Then, he had two of Sinatra's bodyguards escort me off the property.

Two days later, I got a letter from Davis' attorney, informing me that he'd obtained a restraining order that said I had to stay away from his client forever.

As always, there was a conspiracy afoot to prevent me from revealing this absolutely true story.

Harry Pennypacker as a young man. When he wasn't looking for a hot story, he was a dancing king.

Sophie Skulnick in front of her San Francisco home. Her knishes were "to die for".

Little Mendel Skulnick. They say he was a terror with his lasso and slingshot.

This is, ostensibly, one of little Mendel's earliest disguises once he started playing around with his father's magic make-up kit.

Before he became John Wayne, Mendel tried his best to become a cowboy star on his own. This is the last known picture of him, prior to him adopting his more famous visage.

Harry Pennypacker (with guitar) and Oscar Agnew in a Mexican bar. Harry could never understand why the patrons kept throwing empty bottles at him.

Harry Pennypacker and Dr. Sam Hoffman in Las Vegas. Hoffman, a plastic surgeon, offered to fix Harry's broken nose free-of-charge, but after hearing the doctor's story, Harry refused.

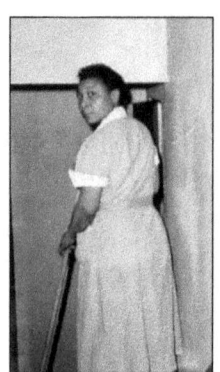

Miss Matilda Webster, Harry Pennypacker's maid. She swore until her dying day that Clark Gable and Hattie McDaniel were *not* lovers.

Howard K. Willoughby. When he wasn't running around in Mae West drag, he liked to wear his little mustache.

Corporal Tommy Lee Oglethorpe, who was part of the U.S. Army commando raid on the Land of Oz. He claims to have personally mowed down six of the Munchkins.

Frightened by Harpo Marx when she was a small child, Gertrude Plotz could never watch a Marx Brothers movie. On one occasion when she had gone to see another picture, the trailer for *Horse Feathers* caused her to rush from the theater screaming.

Jacob Birnbaum was committed to a mental institution for reasons that are unclear. Was it because he thought he was Theodore Roosevelt, or because he knew the truth about Harpo Marx?

Lance Dawson, the man who refuses to admit that Marilyn Monroe was really a female impersonator.

v

W. C. FIELDS & MAE WEST

★

How can somebody be two people at once?

If you don't have to be at the same place at the same time, it's certainly possible.

What if you maintained those dual identities for an entire lifetime?

More difficult, but still possible.

What if both of these people were famous movie stars?

Even more difficult, but it can be done.

But, what if these two great stars were appearing in the same movie, and had many scenes together?

Now, that's were the magic of movies comes into play.

W. C. Fields and Mae West were two of the movies' greatest stars during Hollywood's Golden Era of the 1930s and 40s. Each had their own outrageous comedic style that often bordered on "indecency" and kept censors awake at night. They even co-starred in a film together, 1940's *My Little Chickadee*.

And yet, believe it or not, W. C. Fields and Mae West were the same person.

Mae West was really W. C. Fields in drag, at least, most of the time.

Those other times, when Fields was working elsewhere, she was Howard K. Willoughby.

When Mae West died in 1980, it was rumored that she was really, in fact, a man.

Those weren't rumors.

True, they've never been officially acknowledged, but a week after Mae died, I did speak to Otto Gondorf, who worked as a janitor at the Los Angeles County Coroner's Office, and he told me:

"There were three nude bodies lying on the autopsy tables. One of them was supposed to be Mae West. But, I couldn't tell which was which, because they all had a penis."

Unfortunately, Gondorf only had time to view the genitalia of the three corpses. He was interrupted by the Medical Examiner before he could actually look at their faces, but he *was* "told" that Mae West's body was in that room.

Also, unfortunately, Gondorf had recently emigrated from Europe. He had never seen a Mae West movie, so he really didn't know what she looked like. Worse yet, he was fired that same day for excessive drinking on the job.

That's why he came to me. He figured I might pay him a finder's fee if the story panned out.

I know. Gondorf's testimony is definitely suspect.

Certainly it's not worth the ten dollars I gave him. But, before you dismiss this story completely, let me start from the beginning, and I think that everything will become crystal clear.

William Claude Fields was born in West Philadelphia in 1880. He ran away from home when he was eleven-years-old, after his father smashed him in the head with a shovel.

Not to be outdone, before he left, little William Claude dropped a heavy wooden crate on his father's head, knocking the old son-of-a-bitch out cold.

Out in the world on his own, the lad became fascinated with the art of juggling and decided to take it up as a profession. Unfortunately, it took him awhile to get the hang of it, which explains why he had such a large bulbous red nose.

Some people claim that Fields was born with that unsightly proboscis. Others say he earned it in a series of street fights during his younger days. And, still others insist that it developed because of his love of the bottle.

The truth is that he was such a lousy juggler at first that the boxes he was tossing up into the air kept falling onto his nose and breaking it.

Fields, eventually, perfected his juggling skills and developed a successful vaudeville act that soon became more comedy than juggling.

He also shortened his name to "W.C. Fields", because it was easier to fit onto a marquee.

Later, after hearing all the "Water Closet" jokes, he would regret using those initials.

As history tells us, Fields went on to work for Ziegfeld, made silent movie comedies and, when talkies came in, he perfected his public persona as the rascally, irascible curmudgeon who hated children [he preferred them *"fried"*] and never had anything good to say about the proud, the pious and all the little annoyances in our malicious world that plagued him daily.

However, somewhere along the line, Fields got the idea for a new, somewhat scandalous, line of comedy.

The problem was that this type of humor would not work within the confines of the W.C. Fields character that his audiences had come to know.

This humor was, in fact, better suited for a woman.

After all, what man would come out with a line like:

"Is that a gun in your pocket? Or, are you just glad to see me?"

Or, even better:

"It's not the man in your life that counts. It's the life in your man."

Fields wasn't about to sell his material so that somebody else could take credit for it. Thus, he decided to create a second persona for himself.

Fields figured that he would disguise himself as a woman and do all of this new sexually suggestive material himself.

The problem was that Fields was an ugly bastard.

Any woman who even looked the slightest bit like him might

be attractive to a horse or a chimpanzee, but certainly not to a human being.

The comedian realized that, in order to make his plan work, he would have to do a complete makeover.

Plastic surgery was out. So was a sex change.

What did he do?

Remember Mendel Skulnick?

I discovered that Fields and Mendel used to eat breakfast at the same coffee shop off Hollywood Boulevard. They became friendly around the time that Mendel was designing his John Wayne body suit.

Mendel told Fields about his project and the comedian made him an offer that he couldn't refuse.

[No, he didn't put a gun to Mendel's head. This wasn't *The Godfather*.]

Fields offered to pay all of Mendel's living expenses while he constructed his John Wayne body suit *if* he would also create a body suit for him.

Since Mendel was then living on his mother's "care packages" from San Francisco, he certainly couldn't turn this offer down.

"What kind of body suit do you want?" he asked Fields.

"I want to be the most beautiful, sexy woman on the planet," Fields said.

Mendel studied Fields for a long moment, and then replied, "I can't do the impossible."

Fields started to fume. "Godfrey Daniel!" he said.

[*Actually, he didn't say that exactly, but I'm trying to keep this book suitable for a family audience.*]

"What *can* you do for me?" Fields asked.

"I can make you somewhat attractive," Mendel said, "but definitely not beautiful. And, you'll be a bit *zaftig*."

"*Zaftig*?" Fields asked.

"Plump, buxom."

"That'll work," Fields said.
Enter Mae West.

You might be wondering how I know about this secret alliance between Fields and Mendel Skulnick.

Remember Emile Greenbaum, Mendel's neighbor?

"I saw W.C. Fields in Mendel's apartment two or three times.

"Mendel usually kept his door open. I'd walk by, and there would be Fields, standing in his underwear, straw boater on his head, smoking a cigar, while Mendel was measuring his arms, his legs, with a tape measure.

"I asked Mendel one day, 'What are you doing with Fields with all that measuring?'

"'I'm making him a suit,' he said, then he shut the door.

"A few weeks later, I was walking down the hallway. Mendel's door was open, so I glanced inside, and I couldn't believe what I saw.

"There was Fields, his straw boater on his head, smoking his cigar, wearing a dress. But, the strange thing was that he had a woman's body, breasts, big ass...

"Mendel saw me. Slammed the door in my face.

"Then, I realized what was going on. They were a couple of faygelehs, doing what faygelehs do, whatever that is.

"I wasn't really surprised. After all, they were in show business."

What Greenbaum witnessed, of course, was *not* two gay men doing what gay men do, but Mendel fitting Fields into the body suit that would, eventually, turn him into Mae West.

And, while Mendel was doing his work, Fields was taking voice and body movement lessons, so that when he launched his new persona, he would be convincing as a female.

The late Madame Olga Katrina was Fields' voice and movement coach. In her unpublished autobiography, she wrote:

"W.C. Fields was my greatest success. When he began working with

me, he was an absolute clod. But, when he was finished, he could have danced *Swan Lake*.

"He would have danced it badly, but he could have danced it."

When he was satisfied with all aspects of his Mae West persona, Fields secured a vaudeville booking in order to try out his new act in front of an audience.

Mae West and her sexually suggestive, albeit humorous, routine was an instant hit with vaudeville audiences.

Flo Ziegfeld, not realizing that he was really talking to Fields, even asked her to join his *Follies*.

She turned the showman down in favor of a movie deal with Paramount Pictures, which, not so coincidentally, also had W.C. Fields under contact.

Mae's first picture was *Night After Night* with George Raft.

Raft, who was a nice man, but certainly not the sharpest knife in the drawer, was quite taken with his new, buxom and quite outspoken leading lady. He asked her out on a date.

She refused, but he persisted. She kept turning him down.

Then, one evening, after filming that day on the picture had finished, Raft was strolling past Mae's dressing room. The door was ajar. He glanced inside and blanched.

There was Mae, her back to the door, sitting in her costume with her feet up on the dressing table. She was wearing a straw boater, had a cigar in one hand and a pint of bourbon in the other.

She was talking to somebody, who was out of Raft's eyesight. At least he figured that there was another person in the room with her, because he heard two voices, and one of them belonged to a man.

Then, he recognized the man's voice. It was W.C. Fields.

Was Mae West having an affair with W.C. Fields?

Raft figured that she had to be. Otherwise, why would she be wearing Fields' boater and smoking a cigar?

Anybody who would sleep with W.C. Fields was not for him, so George never asked Mae out again.

Mae West quickly became a big star, which created a major problem for Fields.

How could he be both W.C. Fields and Mae West at the same time?

Creating a fictional background for Mae West was not an issue, since studio publicity departments did that all the time.

Scheduling work dates, so that a Fields movie would wrap before a West movie began shooting and vice versa, was also fairly easy to accomplish.

What did *not* offer an easy solution was when both Fields and West were required to appear at the same premiere, party or other public event.

That's when Howard K. Willoughby entered the picture.

Willoughby was a drinking buddy of Fields and, because they were virtually the same size, he sometimes acted as the comedian's stand-in on movie sets.

Ultimately, since he could easily slip into the body suit, Willoughby also became Fields' stand-in for Mae West.

In order to pull off this double charade, Fields arranged for his friend to have lessons from Madame Olga Katrina, so that in his limited appearances as Mae, he would be able to approximate her voice and movements.

Madame Katrina: *"Mr. Willoughby did his best. He was able to impersonate the Mae West voice adequately, but he would never be able to dance* Swan Lake. *Not even badly."*

The truth is that Willoughby's first public appearance as Mae West was almost a total disaster.

To be fair, Willoughby was forced to attend a premiere before he'd been totally trained in the Mae West phraseology, and he panicked. Every time somebody asked him a question, he replied with the only Mae West phrase he'd mastered: "Come up and see me sometime."

Over time, the masquerades perfected themselves with few, if any problems. Fields continued to play West on film and in her solo public appearances, while Willoughby assumed the role on other occasions when both Fields and West were required to be present.

Willoughby even lived in the secluded, well-guarded residence that belonged to Mae West.

The deceptions worked so well that, in 1940, Fields agreed to co-star in a movie with Mae West, *My Little Chickadee*. He would, of course, play both roles (for a double salary), and co-write the script with Ms. West (also for a double salary).

Director Edward Cline and very few others were in on the Fields/West deception. Those that were were sworn to secrecy, which, if violated, would mean that they would never work in Hollywood again.

How were the scenes between West and Fields accomplished?

By the same tried-and-true method that, in other movies, allowed stars like Bette Davis, Olivia de Havilland, Boris Karloff and Danny Kaye to play their own twins.

It was a combination of cinematic double-exposure and a body double who, in *My Little Chickadee*, was Howard K. Willoughby.

W.C. Fields died in 1946.

That left Howard K. Willoughby with a major problem.

Mae West was his bread-and-butter, but without Fields, how could his masquerade continue?

After all, W.C. Fields *was* Mae West.

Then, suddenly, Willoughby realized that he didn't have a problem at all.

He had the Mae West body suit.

He was living in West's very secluded house.

He also had access to West's vast fortune, since Fields had set up several bank accounts and a safety deposit box filled with cash in Mae's name as a way to lower his income taxes.

Mae West had, essentially, retired from the screen in 1943, so there was no longer any need to perform in public.

If Howard was careful, he could be Mae West for the remainder of his life.

And, that's what he did.

In the 1970s, Mae West did star in two more movies.

Nobody realized that it was really Howard K. Willoughby performing in that now slightly cracked body suit. He had spent the past thirty years working with vocal, acting and movement coaches, and any deviation from Fields' original characterization was attributed to the fact that Mae West had just gotten older.

I only wish that Otto Gondorf, the janitor at the Los Angeles Coroner's Office, had taken a camera into that autopsy room.

Then, I would have absolute proof that the story I've just related to you is true.

VI

THE WIZARD OF OZ

★

Remember *The Wizard of Oz*? Remember how you hummed along with Judy Garland, Ray Bolger, Jack Haley and Bert Lahr, as they skipped down the Yellow Brick Road on their way to the Emerald City?

A wonderful movie, wasn't it?

It's one that you and your children and your grandchildren will enjoy forever.

Would you believe that the Land of Oz actually existed?

In fact, despite what you may have read in the history books, the 1939 movie classic was actually filmed on location in the Land of Oz.

Stories that the picture was shot at the MGM studio were a complete fabrication, and I can prove that.

How do I know?

A Munchkin told me.

I've also uncovered evidence that the Land of Oz was completely destroyed by the United States Government near the end of the Second World War.

Like the destruction of our Native Americans, this was a shameful episode in our nation's history. It resulted in what was probably the biggest Government cover-up prior to the alien creatures from Mars landing in Roswell, New Mexico.

Frank L. Baum, who wrote *The Wizard of Oz*, discovered that magical land near the end of the 19th-century when he was visiting friends in New Mexico. It was located inside of a remote mesa outside Alamogordo.

According to legend, Baum stopped his wagon near the mesa in order to take a leak. He let go against what appeared to be an old metal boiler, but as soon as he was in full stream, the "boiler" let out a yelp, jumped up and shouted, *"What the fuck do you think you're doing?"*

Baum couldn't believe his eyes.

Standing before him was a man made completely of tin. He'd been taking a nap and he was fighting mad.

Baum fainted dead away, and when he awoke a couple of hours later, he found himself surrounded by Munchkins in Munchkinland.

Baum was immediately made to feel welcome by the happy Munchkins, the affable Scarecrow, the overly friendly Lion and, once he'd wiped himself off, the Tin Man. Even the Wizard performed some card tricks for him.

The author was totally dazzled by the riches of Oz, particularly it's 18-karat gold Yellow Brick Road and it's capital city built with huge emeralds.

The people of Oz allowed Baum to write about their land, providing he kept its location a secret. He agreed and, over the next few years, he wrote not only *The Wizard of Oz*, but also thirteen sequels.

Baum died in 1919, and the location of the Land of Oz was buried with him.

Years went by. In the late 1930s, MGM decided to film *The Wizard of Oz* with director Mervyn LeRoy as its producer.

LeRoy had heard rumors that the Land of Oz was a real place, so he sent the studio's location managers to investigate. The search took several weeks, but the men were finally able to locate the fabled land inside of the Alamogordo mesa.

After intense negotiations, the citizens of Oz agreed to let Leroy shoot the film on location in their land, under two conditions:

1. In order to keep the location of Oz secret, all publicity about the film would state that it was actually shot at the MGM studios in Culver City, California.
2. MGM contract players Joan Crawford and Myrna Loy

would join the Wizard one night for a romantic threesome while the Scarecrow watched.

So, the movie was shot, released and the rest, as they say, is history.

Actually, some of the Munchkins were so taken with the moviemaking process that they left Oz when filming was completed and moved to Hollywood. One of them was Wilbur Rathbone (no relation to Basil), who, until his death in 1972, worked regularly in motion pictures, doubling for child actors. He's the person who turned me on to this amazing story.

"Judy Garland and I were lovers," he claimed, one spring day in 1963 when I met him at the Raincheck, a popular bar on Santa Monica Boulevard. He had recently been released from a mental health facility.

"Our affair began while we were making the picture in Oz," he claimed. *"At night, instead of staying at the Alamogordo Hotel with the rest of the film company, Judy would sneak over and stay with me in my little cottage in Munchkinland.*

"We even talked about marriage, but when I came to Hollywood and tried to see her, they wouldn't let me into the studio."

Representatives of Judy Garland's estate denied that the late star ever knew anybody named Wilbur Rathbone, but they do acknowledge that she was very fond of Toto.

Now, let's move forward a few years.

It's 1942. The United States is fighting World War II on multiple fronts.

The Manhattan Project is authorized by President Franklin Roosevelt to develop the atomic bomb. Secret headquarters, under the leadership of General Leslie R. Groves, are set up outside of Alamogordo, New Mexico.

It wasn't long before security forces for the base discovered the existence of Oz.

General Groves visited the Land and conferred with the Wizard, who entertained him with some card tricks.

Groves told the Wizard that he and the rest of Oz' population had ninety days to move out of the mesa, because that piece of real estate was destined to be Ground Zero for the first atomic bomb test.

The Wizard refused. "Our people have lived here for centuries," he told Groves, "and we are not going to leave our homes. Besides, where would we go?"

"We could send you up North to live on a reservation with the Cheyenne," Groves said, "or to Florida to share space with the Apaches. We can give you beachfront property and you might even meet some of Geronimo's descendents there."

The Wizard insisted that he and his people were *not* Native Americans, but citizens of the sovereign land of Oz.

"Have it your own way," Groves said, taking in the wonders of the Yellow Brick Road and the Emerald City as he departed.

Groves returned to his headquarters and immediately phoned Washington. "We can scrap the War Bonds drive," he told his superiors. "I've found a better way to pay for our war effort."

Corporal Tommy Lee Oglethorpe was part of a U.S. Army commando raid, carried out in July of 1944, that invaded and destroyed the peaceful Land of Oz. He heard that I'd been making inquiries about Oz and called me. I interviewed him at the Los Angeles Veterans Hospital shortly before his death in 1969.

Corporal Oglethorpe: *"Our mission was to repel down into the mesa, grab up all them 18-karat gold bricks from the Yellow Brick Road and the emeralds from the Emerald City, then get the hell out of there.*

"Nobody was supposed to get hurt, but then that bunch of Commies, the Lollipop Guild, started comin' at us, and we had to open fire. Mowed them little guys down like a bunch of bowling pins.

"Then, the rest of those crazy creatures started for us. The worst of them was the flyin' monkeys. They'd swoop down, bat one of us guys on the head then take off. Good thing some of us had anti-aircraft training. Otherwise, we might not've been able to shoot 'em down.

"It took a bazooka to blow apart that tin guy, but that Commie made from straw went up with one quick blast from my flame-thrower. Whoosh!

"That Wizard guy, he got away. Took off in a hot air balloon for places unknown. Think he was headed west"

According to the Corporal, the only other survivor from the Land of Oz was a lion, who hid in a corner during the entire battle. He was later sent to live in the St. Louis Zoo.

And, as for the Wizard, some say he wound up in Hollywood, waiting tables at the old Brown Derby restaurant on Vine Street. Others claim he was one of the founding members of the Magic Castle.

Still others insist that the Wizard was so angry at the United States for its betrayal that, before he set off in his balloon, he grabbed a bunch of seeds from the deadly poppy field and set sail for Asia. As he flew over Afghanistan, he let go of those seeds, which was the start of the opium industry that flourishes in that land-locked country today.

In July of 1945, the first atomic bomb was tested on the mesa that once housed the Land of Oz, wiping out all traces of that magical place forever.

I'm sure that I don't have to tell you why our government does not want this embarrassing story to get out, nor why my editor buried it.

VII

THE MARX BROTHERS

★

If you think the United States Government wanted to keep what happened to the Land of Oz quiet, that was nothing compared to the ultra high, eyes only, red alert, burn after reading, top secret that surrounded The Marx Brothers.

That's right!

The Marx Brothers. Groucho, Chico and, most especially, Harpo.

You thought I meant Karl Marx?

If you think that the first landing of alien beings on this planet occurred in 1947 in Roswell, New Mexico, you are very much mistaken.

That historic event actually took place back around 1895, on the beach at Coney Island.

Leonard and Julius, two little Jewish boys, were playing in the surf when they came across a strange-looking, happy little creature about three feet tall. It had wide googley eyes, a huge wild growth of what appeared to be blonde hair on its head and, when it opened its mouth, the only sound that came out was "Beep! Beep!"

The boys attempted to shake hands with the creature, but instead of extending his hand, the thing lifted his leg and let them grab hold of it.

Leonard and Julius were delighted with their new friend. They spent the afternoon playing in the sand, building sand castles.

Actually, Leonard and Julius were building the sand castles. The little creature was building this elaborate round, saucer-like object that had doors, windows and what appeared to be some sort of an engine on its top.

Whenever Leonard or Julius would ask him what he was building, the creature just answered with a "Beep! Beep!"

At the end of the day, the boys brought their new friend over to their mother, Minnie, who had been knitting and napping up the beach. She was a bit taken aback when she saw the strange little creature, but being a kind-hearted woman, she smiled and extended her hand.

He gave her his leg.

After shaking his leg, Minnie asked, "And, where is your mommy and daddy?"

The creature looked a bit forlorn and pointed skyward.

"Oh, you poor little thing," Minnie, said, tears forming in her eyes. She held her large arms out to the creature and embraced him. "Such a sad, sad life."

Leonard and Julius beamed. "Mama," they said, "can we keep him?"

Minnie looked at the creature. "You have no place to go?" she asked.

Still looking forlorn, lower lip extended, the creature shook his head.

"Then you will come home with us," Minnie said. "Do you have a name?"

"Beep! Beep!" replied the creature.

"We can't call you that," Minnie said. She thought for a moment. "I had an uncle who had wide eyes like yours," she continued. "His name was Arthur. How about we call you 'Arthur'?"

A big smile broke out on the creature's face. He nodded enthusiastically.

"Then, Arthur it is," Minnie said, taking the creature's hand and leading him off the beach with Leonard and Julius tagging along behind.

Thus, what was the first "E.T." became a member of the Marx Family that resided on New York's Lower East Side.

In case you're wondering how I know this, the scene I just described to you was witnessed by Gertrude Plotz, who was four-years-old at the time. She was playing on the beach a few feet away from the Marx boys and the creature that afternoon.

"I remember it just like it was yesterday," Gertrude told me when I visited her in a Cleveland Nursing Home shortly before she died. *"I was sitting on the beach, digging a big hole in the sand, when all of a sudden, I heard this big 'plop' next to me.*

"I turned around and there, a couple of feet away from me, was this very weird-looking person who hadn't been there before. I guess it was a person. He had these big funny eyes and like a jungle of blonde hair on his head. And, I'm not sure, but there might have been a couple of pointy things sticking out from under his hair, just above his forehead.

"He scared me. I started crying. Ran to my mother. She gave me a swat on my bottom. Said I was making too much noise"

Gertrude wasn't the only person to notice the "pointy things" on the newly dubbed "Arthur Marx's" head, but I'll get to that later.

As the world knows, Minnie Marx, who was married to a hard-working tailor, was the world's greatest stage mother. If it weren't for her, there would have been no Marx Brothers. She's the one who pushed her sons to go on stage and she did everything humanly possible to insure their success.

Julius who, when Minnie started handing out stage names, became Groucho, didn't really want to become a performer. He wanted to be a writer.

And, Chico (i.e. Leonard) was more interested in chasing girls and shooting crap. As a gambler, he probably lost as much or more than he won. When he was broke, he'd pawn things. He pawned his father's tailoring shears, his grandfather's walking cane and, on one occasion, he even tried to pawn Arthur.

Arthur, on the other hand, was very pliable. Like any foundling, he wanted to please everybody he met, but his only *real* friends were his brothers.

Since he was so "different" from the other kids, he didn't get along well in school. He was constantly bullied, so he stopped going when he was still in elementary school. Getting dropped regularly out a first story window was not much fun and, next year, his classroom was going to be on the second floor.

The Marx family tried to help Arthur hide his obvious physical differences. They gave him a battered top hat to cover his wild hair and those "pointy things", plus a long, full overcoat that almost extended down to his ankles.

Chico, always trying to work a new crooked angle, saw possibilities in Arthur's big coat.

He had the unknowing Arthur follow him into department stores and, when people weren't looking, he'd grab a piece of merchandise off the counter and stick it into one of his adopted brother's large pockets.

Floor walkers and store detectives may have suspected Chico of shoplifting, because he *did* have that shifty look about him, but Arthur with his wide-eyed expression of innocence was above suspicion. Indeed, after a couple of hours of collecting merchandise that would later be pawned, Arthur would walk out of the store with his pockets bulging, while the store detectives were still following Chico.

On one occasion, a store detective did approach Arthur and ask what he was doing there. The adopted Marx looked at the man with a blank stare, and went "Beep! Beep!" The guy just stood there, mouth agape, as Arthur walked out of the store.

Now, you know the origins of one of The Marx Brothers' most famous movie routines, the overcoat with the pockets that are always full.

Aside from the bent top hat and the overcoat, Minnie also got Arthur a little horn, which he always carried with him. She figured that, since he couldn't talk, it would explain the "Beep! Beep!"

Arthur may not have been able to talk, but he could communicate *when he played the harp*. One day, he found Minnie's grandmother's old harp in the attic of the tenement where they lived, and he started playing it as if he'd been doing it for twenty years.

I'm told by folks who knew Arthur that, when he was caressing those strings, the people he cared about knew what he was saying.

By this time, you must have figured out that "Harpo" was the stage name that Minnie gave her newfound son.

Before he passed away, Jacob Birnbaum, who lived in the apartment below the Marx family for many years, spent over an hour with me when I visited him at the New Jersey State Mental Institution.

"The whole family was meshugge," said Birnbaum. *"That Groucho would never give you a straight answer. Chico was a world-class* gonif, *and that Harpo was something from another planet."*

"Another planet," I asked. "What do you mean?"

"He was the strangest-looking person you ever saw. Wide, crazy eyes. Big bushy blonde hair. And, he had these 'pointy things', like little antennas, sticking out of his head just above his forehead."

"You're saying, he had antennae?"

"He had somethin'," Birnbaum said. *"Hell, he never talked. Just said 'Beep! Beep!' and if you tried to shake hands with him, he'd just give you his leg.*

"The one thing I will say for him is that he played the most beautiful music on the harp. But, that was strange, too."

"How so?" I asked.

"He'd be sitting there, playing away. His mother and brothers would be listening, but they'd be talking at the same time. It was like they were talking to the harp, the harp was talking back and they understood what the harp was saying.

"They got harp music and I got a 'Beep! Beep!' How do you like that?"

I wondered aloud if Birnbaum had ever discussed his impressions of Harpo Marx with anybody else.

"Why do you think I'm in this place," he said. *"I'm not the one who's meshugge.*

"You remember that Orson Welles Man from Mars thing back in 1938? Such a mishegoss *it caused."*

He was referring to that ultra realistic Halloween radio broadcast of H.G. Wells' *The War of the Worlds* that had frightened listeners around the country.

"What about it?" I asked.

"Two weeks after it happened, some Government men knocked on my door and asked me some questions about Harpo Marx. I told them exactly what I told you.

"Next thing I know, they grab me by the arms, throw a straight jacket on me and bring me here, and here I've been ever since."

According to the hospital records, Birnbaum had been committed to the state institution because he claimed he was Teddy Roosevelt. That was okay, but four or five times a day, he'd race up the stairs of his six-floor tenement building, yelling "Charge!" He claimed he was charging up San Juan Hill.

Apparently, the neighbors didn't like that.

[Is it possible that playwright Joseph Kesselring lived in that tenement building?

Was the character of Theodore Brewster in his hit play, *Arsenic and Old Lace*, inspired by Jacob Birnbaum?

Just asking.]

Birnbaum may have been nuts, but that didn't mean he was crazy, at least about Harpo Marx.

I decided to investigate his story further.

By 1938, The Marx Brothers were a show business phenomenon. With their zany antics, they'd conquered vaudeville, Broadway and, now they were the toast of Hollywood, having starred in such hits as *Animal Crackers, Horse Feathers, Duck Soup, A Night at the*

Opera and *A Day at the Races*. Originally, Minnie's two other sons, Gummo and Zeppo, had been part of the act, but now there was just Groucho, Chico and Harpo.

Strangely, the silent Harpo, who had quit school early, became the darling of New York's literary elite that gathered at the fabled "Round Table" at the Algonquin Hotel. Luminaries like Dorothy Parker, Alexander Woollcott, George S. Kaufman, Robert Benchley and others sought his company.

And, why not?

Harpo was different. He was unique. He was friendly. He was funny. And, though these famous folk may not have known it, he was from another planet.

Nobody was ever quite sure what planet Harpo came from, but based on his limited vocabulary, astronomers believed it was the planet *Beepon*, which is in a galaxy far, far away.

How did he get here?

Again, we don't know. Perhaps he was the product of an illegitimate birth and was dropped off on Earth by his mother to avoid scandal.

It was the Orson Welles *War of the World* broadcast that made the United States Government aware of Harpo's existence.

Harpo was furious at Welles and the entire furor that that broadcast created.

That broadcast was *anti-alien*!

It portrayed aliens as vicious, murdering monsters, causing people to be afraid of beings from another planet.

Harpo was from another planet.

He wasn't vicious.

He was funny.

Harpo couldn't speak, but he *could* write. He wrote a letter to President Franklin D. Roosevelt, objecting to the way that Welles had slandered aliens, like himself. He demanded that a law be passed to protect him and others like him from such abuse.

Next day, Harpo opened his front door and came face-to-face with F.B.I. Director J. Edgar Hoover.

The short, bulldog-faced Hoover explained to Harpo that it was necessary to keep the fact that he was from another planet secret, lest it cause a nationwide panic. The public, after all, was afraid of aliens.

Hoover and President Roosevelt knew that Harpo was a friendly alien and posed no threat to the United States. They would certainly not try to deport him back to *Beepon* or wherever he came from, because he was so beloved by his fans that, if he disappeared, too many questions would be asked.

Harpo agreed that he would keep quiet about where he came from, and Hoover told him that he would make sure that his secret remained secret.

The pair shared a couple of drinks together, and then Hoover confided to Harpo that he was from an alien planet, too.

How do I know this?

I used to have a confidential source at the FBI. He was the one who gave me the original tip on Harpo Marx's secret.

He was fired from the Bureau when they caught him peeking inside of Hoover's private files.

According to my source, who has since mysteriously disappeared, in 1947, Harpo took a trip to the Southwest part of the United States. It was my source's guess that he'd been asked by the U.S. Government to visit Roswell, New Mexico, to act as interpreter for the alien beings that had landed there.

What actually occurred there, I don't know.

Harpo quit the movies after the release of The Marx Brothers' 1949 movie, *Love Happy*.

Some people say he was disgusted by the fact that Hollywood was turning out movies like *The Thing*, *Invaders From Mars* and *War of the Worlds*, all of which presented alien beings as vicious, murdering monsters.

Can you blame him?
Shouldn't alien beings have civil rights, too?

Harpo Marx died in 1964.

In 1982, Steven Spielberg came out with his movie, *E.T., The Extra-Terrestrial*.

I've always wondered if Spielberg had somehow stumbled across the story of Harpo Marx's origins and this film was meant to be a homage.

By this time, do I have to tell you why this story never saw print?

VIII
Marilyn Monroe

★

After they killed my stories about Oz and The Marx Brothers, I went to my editors and tried to quit. "If you're not going to run my stuff," I told them, "I'll go someplace else. Maybe, I'll even self-publish."

Unfortunately, my ironclad, life-long contract worked both ways. They couldn't fire me, but also I couldn't quit.

They owned me and everything I wrote.

I continued to write their goddamn TV listings, and I continued to drink, and drink, and drink some more.

One night, I was so drunk, I stumbled into a gay bar.

The patrons were friendly enough, though I think they were wondering what I was doing there. They even bought me a couple of drinks.

While I was sitting at one of the tables, I happened to notice a picture of Marilyn Monroe on the wall, along with photos of Joan Crawford, Bette Davis, Judy Garland and several other famous actresses.

There was something strange about Marilyn's picture. I took a closer look, and suddenly realized that I had, once again, stumbled onto a sensational story, which follows.

She was America's...

Correction! The world's...Number One sex symbol.

Even decades after her death, Marilyn Monroe still reigns supreme.

Yet, a mystery continues to surround her death.

Was it an accident?

Suicide?

Or, was it murder?

And, if it was murder, what was the motive behind it?

I discovered the *real* reason behind Marilyn's death. Unfortunately, the truth was so shocking that it took me years before I could get anybody to talk on the record.

But, eventually, I did find somebody.

His name was Lance Dawson.

He was a small time actor who did a picture with Marilyn.

He also screwed her.

That doesn't really make him unique, since half of Hollywood (and some of Washington D.C.) *claims* to have had sex with her.

The difference is that he was willing to admit it in a taped interview.

Actually, Dawson thought he was coming to my office to audition for a movie. He didn't know the real reason.

I figured I'd ambush him.

As it turned out, I'm the one who got ambushed.

Dawson was a friendly, outgoing guy who spoke like he came from New Jersey.

The truth is that he *did* come from New Jersey, which is why he spoke that way.

He was in his late sixties, a big muscle-bound former boxer with a broken nose; perfect casting for a role in *Little Caesar*, *The Roaring Twenties* or *The Godfather*.

Here is a transcript of our interview, exactly as it took place:

Dawson: *So, what's this role I'm auditioning for?*

Me: *It's an exposé. You're the guy who provides us with the key information.*

Dawson: *Like a stool pigeon, huh?*

Me: *Something like that.*

Dawson: *Never had much use for stoolies, but, I guess, acting is acting. Is it a big part?*

Me: *Central. What roles have you done, Mr. Dawson?*

Marilyn Monroe

Dawson: *Just small parts. I was in a couple of pictures with George Raft. Did a bit in* The Godfather. *Usually, I play somebody's muscle.*

Me: *I can see that.*

[About this time, I was beginning to wonder if I'd made a mistake.]

Me: *I'll bet Lance Dawson isn't your real name.*

Dawson: *Naw. That's my professional handle. Name's Tony Baldovino...from Jersey. My friends call me "Tony Knuckles".*

[Yeah, I was making a mistake. A *big* mistake.]

Me: *I hear you used to be friends with Marilyn Monroe.*

Dawson: *Yeah, I was. She was quite a dame.*

Me: *I hear you were more than friends.*

Dawson: *Yeah, you might say that.*

[I decided to go for it. *Shmuck!*]

Me: *The truth is...you were lovers.*

Dawson: *What is this?*

Me: *It's an exposé, about Marilyn Monroe.*

Dawson: *I don't know who bumped her off, if that's what you mean.*

Me: *No, nothing like that. We just want to know what Marilyn was really like, from somebody who was "intimate" with her.*

Dawson: *I could do that. What do you want to know?*

Me: *Was she a good lover?*

Dawson: *Boy, you really want the goods, don't ya?. Yeah, she was the best. Shy though.*

Me: *What do you mean?*

Dawson: *I always boffed her with the lights off, and her back was always to me. I never once saw that broad naked. She insisted on that.*

Me: *No kidding?*

Dawson: *That's the truth. In fact, you know that famous nude calendar shot of her? The one that was in* Playboy?

Me: *What about it?*

Dawson: *She said that, when the photographer actually took the shot, he was blindfolded. He never saw her bod either.*

Me: *That's amazing. So, you never suspected?*
Dawson: *Suspected what?*
Me: *The truth about Marilyn.*
Dawson: *What truth? She was a great lay.*
Me: *But, she was a man.*
Dawson: *What?*
[He looked like he was going to have a heart attack.]
Me: *Marilyn Monroe was really a female impersonator named Marvin Martinson.*
[He continued to stare at me, mouth agape. He didn't even notice the fly that flew into his mouth, landed on his tongue for a few seconds, and then flew out.]
Me: *That's the reason she was murdered. Too many important men had slept with her (or him), and one of them discovered the truth. He couldn't let that truth get out.*
[Suddenly, I didn't like the expression on Dawson's face.]
Dawson: *You're puttin' this all on tape?*
Me: *Yeah. It's going to be a great story. The story of the century.*
Dawson: *You're puttin' on tape that I fucked a fuckin' fag!?!*
[He stood up, his fists clenched.]
Dawson: *You said I was auditionin' for a goddamn movie.*
Me: *It will be a movie, when my book sells, and you got the key part.*
Dawson: *I don't want the key part. I don't want no part.*
[He made a grab for the cassette recorder, but I snatched it out of his reach.]
Dawson: *I want the fuckin' tape.*
Me: *But, you signed a release.*
[I waved the document in front of him. He snatched it away and ripped it up.]
Dawson: *This fuckin' release is going up your fuckin' ass!*
[He started chasing me around the room.]
Dawson: *Give me that tape.*
[He took hold of my desk, and with seemingly little effort,

tipped it over. Everything on top of it went flying all over the room, paper, pencils, my stapler and my plaster of Paris replica of The Maltese Falcon, which bounced off the back wall and split in two.

[I knew that my neck was going to be next, so I held the cassette recorder out to him.]

Me: *Okay. You can have it. You can have it.*

Dawson: *Damn fuckin' right I can have it.*

[He snatched the recorder away and headed for the door. Then, he turned and walked back toward me. I saw his fist heading toward my face. That's the last thing that I remember.]

The police showed up just as Lance Dawson was leaving and arrested him.

I got the interview tape back, along with a black eye, a bruised-up face and a dislocated right arm.

A fantastic story, right?

But, as usual, nobody would print it.

★

Lance Dawson was sentenced to three years in the state prison for assault and battery.

For the rest of his life, Harry Pennypacker wrote and continuously revised his autobiography.

Sadly, he could not find anyone to publish it because, like his newspaper columns, the stories in it were *too hot*. *Too dangerous*.

Pennypacker died peacefully in his sleep in 1998. He was 87 years old.

At the time, he was living alone in a one-room apartment just off Vermont Avenue in Hollywood.

Scribbled on a notepad next to his bed were two words, "Nessie" and "Tessie".

Stuart Blumberg was sentenced to serve 90 days in the county jail for stealing files from the Los Angeles newspaper library where he'd once worked.

He is now free and seeking financing for a different film, based on Pennypacker's material, in which he will reveal, among other things, that an iceberg did not sink the Titanic.

Blumberg says that Pennypacker had spoken to a survivor of that tragedy.

According to Mrs. Abner Whitford, an eyewitness who had just come out of the ship's cocktail lounge, the Titanic actually collided with "Tessie," the first cousin once-removed of "Nessie," the Loch Ness monster.

Anybody who would like to invest in this new motion picture can contact Mr. Blumberg c/o the publisher of this book.

And, as for me, I've now gone on to another project.

Disclaimer

★

This disclaimer is for the benefit of any reader who may not be the brightest bulb in the chandelier.

What you have just read is a parody, a work of total fiction.

Harry Pennypacker, Stuart Blumberg, Mendel and Sophie Skulnick, Robert T. Atwater, Otis Washington and the other "witnesses" in these stories do not exist. They are all creations from this writer's imagination.

None of the stories about Charles Lindbergh, John Wayne, Lon Chaney, Elvis Presley, James Dean, Clark Gable, Hattie McDaniel, Sammy Davis, Jr., W.C. Fields, Mae West, Judy Garland, Frank Baum, General Leslie Groves, The Marx Brothers, J. Edgar Hoover, Marilyn Monroe or any other actual person is true.

However, if you do insist on believing them, I have a couple of bridges, one in San Francisco and the other in Brooklyn, that are for sale.

★

Now that I've come clean and admitted that this book is a total fiction, you're probably wondering about the photographs in the center section.

If they're not Harry Pennypacker, or Mendel Skulnick or Sophie Skulnick, then who the hell are these people?

I'm not going to give you a complete cast of characters, but Harry Pennypacker was "played" by my late father, Harry Druxman, Sophie Skulnick by my paternal grandmother, the adult Mendel Skulnick by my maternal grandfather, and little Mendel is *me*.

Like Alfred Hitchcock, I had to do a "walk-on".

The rest of the cast are various friends and family members, as well as my first dog (Bonnie), none of whom are with us any longer.

The very talented Dave Woodman drew the caricatures and front cover for this book. You can view more of Dave's work by visiting:

www.theWonderfulWorldofWoodman.com

Dedication

★

To all the great stars who will continue to shine bright in the Hollywood heavens, despite the affectionate satire contained in this book.

And, to Harry Pennypacker and Mendel Skulnick, wherever they are.

ABOUT THE AUTHOR

★

Michael B. Druxman is a veteran Hollywood screenwriter whose credits include *Cheyenne Warrior* with Kelly Preston, *Dillinger and Capone* starring Martin Sheen and F. Murray Abraham and *The Doorway* with Roy Scheider, which he also directed.

He is also a prolific playwright, his one-person play, *Jolson*, having had numerous productions around the country.

Additionally, he is the author of twelve other published books, including several non-fiction works about Hollywood, it's movies and the people who make them (e.g. *Basil Rathbone: His Life and His Films*, *Make It Again, Sam: A Survey of Movie Remakes*), plus two novels, *Nobody Drowns in Mineral Lake* and *Shadow Watcher*.

A native of Seattle, Mr. Druxman currently resides in Los Angeles with his wife, Sandy.

www.ingramcontent.com/pod-product-compliance
Lightning Source LLC
Chambersburg PA
CBHW071624170426
43195CB00038B/2092